Roses are Silent

Bara wa Shizuka

Tamiko Dooley

Previously by Tamiko Dooley

SHIMA (Islands),
published by Alien Buddha Press, 2022

Seasons of Love Around the Rising Sun,
published by Broken Sleep Books, 2023

The Japanese House,
published by Cephalo Press, 2023

Gakusei (The Schoolgirl),
published by Nat 1 LLC, 2024

Roses are Silent

Bara wa Shizuka

Tamiko Dooley

Black Eyes Publishing UK

Roses are Silent
© Tamiko Dooley, 2025

First published in 2025
Black Eyes Publishing UK
Gloucester
United Kingdom

www.blackeyespublishinguk.co.uk

ISBN: 978-1-913195-30-4

Tamiko Dooley has asserted her moral right under the Copyright, Designs and Patents Act, 1988, to be identified as the author of this work.

All Rights reserved. No part of this publication may be reproduced, copied, stored in a retrieval system, or transmitted, in any form or by any means, without the prior written consent of the copyright holder, nor be otherwise circulated in any form of binding or cover other than that in which it is published and without a similar condition being imposed on the subsequent purchaser.

A CIP catalogue record for this title is available from the British Library.

Edited by: Josephine Lay

Cover: Jason Conway, The Daydream Academy
www.thedaydreamacademy.com

Dedication

To the tutors and alumni of New College, Oxford:
"Manners Makyth Man"

UERU (Planting)

13 Tsuru (Crane)
14 My Irish grandmother solves The Times cryptic crossword puzzle
16 Yuyake (sunset)
17 Omiyage (A Gift)
18 My Japanese cousins teach me *Yakuza* slang
20 Ki (Tree)
21 Kakurembo (Hide and Seek)
22 Recording

SAKU (Blooming)

27 Eros: sorE
28 Ayatori (Cat's Cradle)
29 Slipstream
30 Sampo (A walk)
31 Ohanami
32 Being brave
33 Examination
34 Yume (Dreams)

SASU (Pricking)

39 Red Shoes (Akai Kutsu)
40 Nomikai (After work drinks)
41 Cyanotype by Amidaiji-jingu
42 Tsukareta? (You Must Be Tired)
43 Daruma-san
44 Momo (peach)

45 Shower Time
46 Joya no Kane (New Year's Eve Bell)
47 Anata (You)
48 Piano Lesson

KIRU (Deadheading)

53 When Matisse saved Uncle Chiaki's life
54 Ensoku (School trip)
55 The House (Uchi)
56 Wildlife
57 alumni weekend
58 Lake Yamanaka
59 Reunion
61 Unboxing

65 Glossary
67 Acknowledgements
69 Tamiko Dooley
71 Full Quotes

UERU (Planting)

Tsuru (Crane)

Her finger presses clean along the line
Sharp as the edge of his electric bed

Each fold, a prayer
Lips as tight as paper creases

They say the crane has a lifespan of a thousand years

Its wings are symmetrical
Its neck, majestic

She brings the origami to her mouth
Inflates its belly with a gentle blow

Outside, the wind whips up leaves
That drop to the ground

They dance briefly as if of their own accord

The miniature bird sits on the bedside table
Watching as he sleeps

Each fold, a prayer of flight

Of the thousand flights they still wish to take

My Irish grandmother solves The Times cryptic crossword puzzle

Give us one to think about
you say over your shoulder
yellow rubber gloves scraping
potatoes off the china
plunging them into the sink

You walk me through reversals
anagrams, dual meanings
to reveal the clues
those five words hide
every ! and ? relevant

When I ask how you learned to solve them
you say as a child you'd sit
at the mahogany dining table
with the folding legs and the scratched surface

And my great-grandmother in her patched-up pinny
hands raw from washing and cooking for nine *leanaí*
sighs and takes a breather
sits for five minutes without guilt
A moment of rest

where she passes onto my grandmother
the secrets *she* learned as a girl in Ireland
Perhaps to escape the mangle and tub
the hob that explodes with gas when you light it

When my pencil writes in neatly
ERUDITE

I see her handwriting
as if my great-grandmother were penning
the word herself and smiling:
There, you could do it all along
And still onwards she encourages, onto the next clue

Come on, a Stór mo Chroí:
Give us one to think about.

Yuyake (Sunset)

And my Japanese grandmother pedals and pedals
out west to trade
the family's precious kimonos

I follow her to a stranger's house
where she will swap embroidered fabric for *daikon* and *tofu*
And in the early evening she cycles home
facing the sunset

The *yuyake* lights up her cheeks
until they glow amber

As if the heat radiating from Hiroshima
pushes her faster

Gears grinding as she ascends back to Nakano
onwards, onwards towards the setting sun

Omiyage (A Gift)

I drink from the cup
ceramic fired by your hand
my lips are burning

wan kara nomu
kimi no tezukuri
kuchi yakeru

My Japanese cousins teach me Yakuza slang

And at a family meal at a Roppongi restaurant
where the napkins are origami cranes
(but there is Western cutlery to show progress)
my cousins whisper that when I finish
I should shout *"Gotsan deshita!"* which is what gangsters say
when they're done eating

So I yell it at the end of dinner
the whole family roars with laughter
And to feed the lion
more bad words trip off my tongue
everything I've learned from J-dramas during our stay
"Oi, nandazo!"

And through it all I meet the eyes of my mother
Because hasn't she spent my childhood
nurturing someone with whom to speak her mother tongue
whilst she's far from home

And amn't I spreading my wings
by learning new words that aren't hers?
I can't tell what she's thinking at first

But soon her shoulders start to shake
the dirty words lift weights off her
until she's holding her stomach with laughter
My cousins and I wipe tears from our eyes
as we reach for a glass of ice cold *mugicha*
to wash down the meal

And to wash out my mouth
of all that *Yakuza* slang

Ki (Tree)

      my grandmother tells a story from
   when she was little: at the end of her garden in
nakano was a zakuro tree if you plucked the scarlet
      fruit you would pull on the hair of kazuko
            the girl buried under the
               roots and her screams
                   would
                    tear
                     at
                   your
                   ears

Kakurembo (Hide and Seek)

in the *zashiki*, she wants to play
hear her calling
Mou ikai?
waiting… to respond
Mou iyo

Out of the corner you see
glint of scarlet *obi*
swing of a ponytail

turn your head towards
and she's

Recording

if only in our conversations / I could press the pedal / keep your voice going / sustain that bass note / your tone, your timbre / hold my foot to the floor / dampener up / let the string vibrate on and on and

SAKU (Blooming)

Eros:

are you here

again you love

can I see you:

sorE

Ayatori (Cat's Cradle)

my fingers strain
      to hold the next move
string biting into skin
      you pluck and pull
up and over and under
      you take it from me
build your own structure
      together our hands dance
heads close together
      until our skin almost touches
by the end of the game
      you are looking into my eyes
and I do not understand
      the unravelling inside me

Slipstream

Kono kaze, doda!
you exclaimed
jamming both hands into your pockets
shoulders braced against
the early January hours

I wrapped my *hanten* jacket tighter
You walked closely ahead to absorb the gale force

We were trudging away from the Akihabara bar
with its corners that hid the way you looked at me

When we arrived at my apartment in Kamitakada
you turned to face me on the frosted steps
and the winter night

took

        the

air

        out

of

        my

                lungs

Sampo (A walk)

Barefoot

hadashi de

I walked across the moon

tsuki aruita

I was searching for you

kimi sagashiteta

in the crushing darkness

kitsui kurasa de

I couldn't breathe

iki dekinai

When you reached for my hand

boku no te o nigitta

the craters crumbled beneath me

kureta ga kowareta

Ohanami

sakura season
you lay me down on the grass
lips soft as petals

Being brave

The clouds across your face
rumble, threatening to rip the sky
Your mouth trembles from holding firm
face forcing eyes from filling

My promise of treats to rot the teeth
or a trip on the trains
no longer has the power to lift the storm

And in the moment of disappointment disguised
I see that **this** is growing:
not the lines on your wall to mark the months
nor shoes that your toes strain against

but the hiding of pain;
those words that seeped beneath your skin

I grip the protective shield tightly,
yet the armour that once gleamed as lightening
sits tarnished in an ever-loosening fist

Examination

Q: Define "horror"

A: you lie down on the blue paper, legs apart, and it starts THE MOMENT the nurse inserts the speculum and you spend the whole time APOLOGISING as she whispers in alarm

There is a lot of blood

Yume (Dreams)

late at night
I whisper your name into the dark
wrap my lips and teeth
around those unfamiliar sounds
letters that don't belong together
you say your surname is a tongue twister in your language
I lie facing the ceiling, repeating it until
it makes my throat dry
succumbing to echoes of
your name, your name, your name
until sleep takes

SASU (Pricking)

Red Shoes (Akai Kutsu)

If you wear scarlet shoes
you'll marry a gaijin
her father declared

She'd read the grim fairy tale
It was only make-believe –

Yet here she stands aproned
at the sink of her suburban kitchen
Legs intact, but her English marriage wearing thinner
than the soles of those *akai kutsu*

Down the landline, the call short to save the yen
Finger twisting the coil

Didn't I warn you, her father cried

about the shoes

Nomikai (After work drinks)

I don't remember
when the *yuzu* sake was being poured
I don't remember
why we stood alone outside
I don't remember
how we ended up in the taxi
I don't remember
your *genkan*
But I remember
half-falling asleep
I remember
needing help climbing the stairs
I remember
your sweat-soaked face
grinning in half-*kurasa*
And I
Remember
Saying
No

Cyanotype by Amidaiji-jingu

when I lay the leaves, bones
and broken bottles
on the chemical paper
you say the sun will bleach it
mark the outline of the trinkets
I've scavenged off the beach

after a while we lift it from the pebbles

on the dark blue scroll
white X-rays begin to emerge

you see? you smile
leave it out in the open air
it will tell you its history

I wonder if I lie on the paper
you'd see the stains from my past too

I squint up into the Osaka sunshine

will it show my broken heart?

Tsukareta? (You Must Be Tired)

…couldn't sleep last…

   …in sheets damp from…

      …wondering who you…(*dareh to*)…

   …almost taste your…

…I don't even…(*soredemo*)…

      …would never…(*muri muri*)…

      …but you've been running through my…

(*asobini kuru?*)

Daruma-san

I laughed when you said
I resembled a *daruma-san*

Through the smoky air of the *izakaya* bar:
However often you're pushed over
you just bounce back, don't you?

That night, alone
I grimace comically in the mirror

At last the glass reflects
the meaning of your words

With a fist I smash the child's toy
Sweep up the crumbs

to leave no trail behind:

sometimes you have to break
to return to who you used to be

Momo (Peach)

On a summer's day
when I have to squint into the sky
I sink my front teeth into a *momo*
It tastes of you
salt and nectar
One day longer and it would have
overripened. Today, it's just right
but it's not long
until I reach the core
brittle stone scratches the tongue, breaking my molars
I always forget:

the longer I devour the flesh
the harder it hurts when it ends

Shower Time

there are things you learn from
doing the same job every day
tasks you repeat OVER
and over like, aren't we all the same?

plugging in the hose, brushes out
for meticulous scrubbing
pulling hazmat on MY legs
elasticated cap, gloves, rubber boots

nothing to be afraid of
they're already DEAD
pressure-wash down whilst you
blast that Stravinsky, something dramatic
vaseline in the nostrils
doesn't help with the smell

you leave, throw away the suit
it penetrates through

when you shower that night
you sniff it on your skin
so you scour your naked BODY clean
I mean
Isn't that what you've been doing all day, anyway?

Joya no Kane (New Year's Eve Bell)

Fifteen minutes to midnight on *ohmisoka*
We join the crowd leading to Meiji-jingu

In the starless December night
The hollow ring of gongs
Beat through the icy air

Each family ahead
Striking the copper plate
Good luck for the year ahead

The gravel path crunches underfoot
Bodies warm from the huddle
Heading towards the shrine

At the top of the steps
We place our hands on the mallet
I hear someone call my name and turn

You strike the gong
We swing at different times
You forward as I hang back

Before I know it, our turn has ended
You are hurrying down the stone steps
I run to catch up

January already out of sync

I reach for your hand:

It clutches only air

Anata (You)

because even the
                                  way I would
            explain how –

                                                ...without...

      just glancing at –
                            even the scent of –

your hand on the back of
                                  (touched mine?)
                                  (under the *kotatsu*)

when you speak
I read your lips

(I'm drowning)

Piano Lesson

does it have 88 keys, you ask
raising your eyes to mine
and I fall into those icy lakes, shivering

KIRU (Deadheading)

When Matisse saved Uncle Chiaki's life

Tell me how it happened:
the salaryman never takes holidays
but on that day Uncle Chiaki
didn't catch the Chuo line from Nakano to Shinjuku
One day in his corporate lifetime he happened
to have booked to see an exhibition
of Matisse at the Tokyo Met Art Museum
So he drove there
and of all the days in the year
he chose that one
When the Japanese Satellite TV in England
shows commuters panicked or slumped
running as rats through gas-filled underground chambers
choking and crawling
my mother calls home frantically
no-one answers
Because he's standing in the gallery, staring at the Blue Nude
And we say that isn't it strange
tell me how it happened
when others were inhaling toxins and screaming
silence shrouded him, art enveloped him
The provocative lady a *geisha-san's* embrace
irashai, Chiaki-san, dozo
tell me how it happened

Ensoku (School trip)

the boys behind me
on the coach to Odaiba
are playing "kiss, marry, avoid"

Akira is asking
his rapturous audience
which one would you
between Mizuki, Yuna and Tamiko

he keeps explaining the rules
louder and louder
you have to ascribe
one for each, between
Mizuki, Yuna and Tamiko

repeating the same options
for Mizuki, Yuna and Tamiko
I shrink back into the seat
orange velvet scratching at my neck

try to close my ears against
the low murmurings that the boys begin

and I think:
only three girls on this school trip of fifty students
I know which one is assigned to me

The House (Uchi)

And the *tatami* is woven from the hair
of every disobedient child
teeth ground into tea leaves
If you slide open the *shoji*
you can hear feet shuffle down the corridor
away from the light
(doko kana?)
(they're yours)

Wildlife

On Ginza-*dori* road
my eyes and ears are full
of crumbs of conversations
Exposed lightbulbs reflected in puddles

Each interaction between strangers
feeds a spark until the ash starts to glow
until whoosh! a flame burns and keeps the fire alight

Not for me the serenity of pasture, of cows and country
take me on a train into Tokyo, where all about me
strangers pass from station to stop with purpose

Steam erupts from *nezumi*-infested sewers
Each shopkeeper welcomes me with *irashaimase!*
Each offer of free tissue packets in the streets

Because this wildlife feeds me
a jungle where I can breathe
exist among others to become myself

alumni weekend

when the porter lets me in
I pass our old staircase

the painted board lists unfamiliar students
where once our surnames and rooms sat side by side

I try the handle of the junior common room – locked

an old tutor regales us with
funding and finalists, collections and interviews

and I hear the echoes of us as fresh-faced first years
whispering over lines of Soseki, passing notes in Sensei's lectures

until in seconds we are descending the examination hall steps
blinking into sunshine

I let myself out through the back –
the door clicks shut behind me

all that remains are the tones of choristers
hymns from a previous century

wafting through the cloisters into the January air

Lake Yamanaka

when the water lies still
waiting for the day to begin
when a tree with branches bare
stands silent against the frozen sky
in these moments I hear your voice
crisp as early morning grass underfoot
your laugh whips around like January winds
and I reach out towards you:
silent
bare
waiting
still

Reunion

and would it be like the time
we bumped into you at Shinjuku Station
under the giant clock?

you had your wheely suitcase
and were wearing your fluffy *kiroi* cardigan
squinting up at the departure boards

we saw you for a few seconds before you saw us
we skidded across the floor
pushed through crowds towards you
before you could move, before we lost you

your eyes landed on us as we shouted your name
Oba-chan!
your face was one of sunshine, of surprised delight

then with hugs and cheers
we help you with your luggage

what a surprise to see you here!
and where are you going?

I clutch your fragile hands
papery skin over blue-veined bones
as delicate as your *hojicha* tea cups

your watery eyes are a pale December sky

we hold and embrace each other
with the joy that we found you in the city

except this time
we won't wave you off at the platform
but climb aboard the train together
both smiling out the windows
at the fields that pass, that pass and roll into each other
roll on for miles

as far as the train will take us

Unboxing

When she opens the hand-packaged box
with the air mail tags
she unfolds the *Yomiuri Shimbun*
as delicately as if it has been shaped into paper cranes
My grandmother had crumpled up the newspaper to cradle
the *miso*, the *nori*, the *umeboshi*
My mother makes the opening, the reveal, last
as long as she can
a child unfolding a *furoshiki* of clothes at a sleepover
Slowly peel away each layer
Hold each item with the delicacy
with which it was packed
Soon her tears blur the ink in the pages
She pores over the listings of what programmes
are regularly on
which detective shows she is missing
Her fingers touch where my grandmother touched
and they become closer, somehow, in the universe
as if they are standing together, holding hands
across the oceans

END

Glossary

asobini kuru? – do you want to come and play?
daikon – radish
dareh to – with whom
daruma-san – traditional doll, symbol of perseverance
doko kana? – where can she be?
dozo – go ahead
furoshiki – cloth for wrapping clothes, inter alia
gaijin – foreigner
geisha – female entertainer
genkan – front door
hanten – short winter jacket
hojicha – roasted green tea
irashai / irashaimase – come in
izakaya – casual bar serving food
jingu – shrine
kiroi - yellow
kono kaze, doda! – how about this wind!
kotatsu – heated dining table
kurasa - darkness
leanaí – children (Irish)
miso – soy bean paste
mou ikai? – are you ready?
mou iyo – I'm ready
mugicha – barley tea
muri muri – I couldn't possibly
nezumi – mice
nori - seaweed
oba-chan - grandma
obi – kimono belt

ohmisoka – New Year's Eve
oi, nandazo – what's going on
shoji – sliding paper doors
soredemo – even so
Stór mo Chroí – treasure of my heart (Irish)
tatami – woven bamboo floor
umeboshi – dried sour plum
Yomiuri Shimbun – national newspaper
yuyake – sunset
yuzu – citrus fruit
zakuro – pomegranate
zashiki – parlour

Acknowledgements

It has been a pleasure working with Josephine and Peter Lay of Black Eyes Publishing – thank you for your thoughtful edits and publishing of this book. I am also grateful to the reader for choosing this book of poems – I hope you like what you find.

Tamiko Dooley

Tamiko read Latin and French at New College, Oxford. In 2021, she won the BBC Radio 3 carol competition. Her poem "Yurushi" was broadcast as BBC Radio 3's Friday poem in August 2023.

Full Quotes

Tamiko Dooley opens her new collection 'Bara wa Shizuka' with 'Tsuru', about making a crane out of paper, which immediately establishes the cultural context. It is followed by poems about both her Japanese and Irish grandmothers: one sells kimonos, the other is fond of cryptic crosswords. Dooley's poems of love, loyalty, chance and change are themselves a kind of origami, anecdote folded into image, word-sound folded into personal recollection, each given a suggestive shape and delicately balanced between two worlds. As well as glimpses of life in Japan, there are snatches of its language and naturally some haiku (in English and Japanese). Dooley even experiments with macaronic verse. 'Roses are Silent' might be read as a kind of contemporary pastoral. 'Not for me the serenity of pasture, of cows and country,' she writes: 'Take me on a train into Tokyo'.

John Greening, poet, critic and playwright.

Tamiko's poetry keeps evolving and this volume is the perfect reflection of her poetic maturing. The pieces in this book transcend location and straddle across cultures. Each poem is a delicate work that explores the beautiful, fleeting – and sometimes difficult – moments in our daily experience, capturing a unique sensuality that reminds us of the bittersweet nature of life.

Dr Michael Tsang
Programme Director and Lecturer in Japanese Studies,
Birkbeck University

Balanced between languages, cultures and traditions, Tamiko Dooley's 'Roses are Silent' is filled with family memory and the tangled cats' cradles of the sensual world, in all its terror and joy. Whether learning slang from Japanese cousins, working on crosswords with her Irish grandmother, exploring the risks of eating a peach or of going for after work drinks, Dooley and her delicate word music make for a persuasive, propulsive guide.

Adam Horovitz, poet, performer and editor.

Dooley brings an exquisite sense of the potential in different forms – syllabics, prose poetry, technopaignia – to a meditation on lives and loves a world apart. There is both formal mastery here and a sharp, sympathetic sense for human confusion. Tell me how it happened; so she does.

Dr Luke Pitcher, Fellow & Tutor in Classics; Associate Professor in Classical Languages and Literature, Somerville, University of Oxford.

www.ingramcontent.com/pod-product-compliance
Lightning Source LLC
Chambersburg PA
CBHW072106110526
44590CB00018B/3331